Around the
Neighborhood

Mc
Graw
Hill
Education

Contents

Tom Can

Tom can pop the top.

Tom can mop a lot.

Tom can sit on top.

Tom can tap a hot pot.

Can you see Tom in it?

Mom and Nan

Mom can see Nan on top.

Nan can pat a tin pot.

Olivia Bell Photography/Moment/Getty Images

Nan can hop a lot.

Mom can not see Nan.

Can you see Nan on a cot?

Did Dan?

Did Dan see Don on top?

Did Dan see Nan dip it?

Did Dan see Sam mad?

Did Dan see Dot tap?

Did Dan see Dad do it?

Did Sid See Don?

Sad Don can sit and sit.

Can Sid see Don?

Sid can sip and sip.

Sid did tap a pad.

Sid is not sad!

Tip It

Nan and Don do not like it.

Can you go to Tom?

Don can tip it in.

Nan can tip it.

Don and Nan did it!

Week 1 Tom Can

DECODABLE WORDS
Target Phonics Elements
  Initial and Medial Vowel *o:* hot, lot, mop, pop, pot, top, Tom

HIGH-FREQUENCY WORDS
you
Review: a, see, the

Mom and Nan

DECODABLE WORDS
Target Phonics Elements
  Initial and Medial Vowel *o:* on, cot, hop, lot, mom, not, pot, top

HIGH-FREQUENCY WORDS
you
Review: a, and, see

Week 2 Did Dan?

DECODABLE WORDS
Target Phonics Elements
  Initial and Final *d:* Dan, Dad, did, dip, Don, Dot, mad

HIGH-FREQUENCY WORDS
do
Review: see

Did Sid See Don?

DECODABLE WORDS
Target Phonics Elements
  Initial and Final *d:* did, Don, pad, sad, Sid

HIGH-FREQUENCY WORDS
do
Review: a, and, see

Week 3 Tip It

DECODABLE WORDS
Target Phonics Elements
  Review Initial and Medial *i:* it, in, did, tip; **Initial and Final *n:*** Nan, in, not, can, Don; **Initial *c:*** can; **Initial and Medial *o:*** Don, not; **Initial and Final *d:*** did, Don

HIGH-FREQUENCY WORDS
and, do, go, to, you
Review: like

HIGH-FREQUENCY WORDS TAUGHT TO DATE
Grade K
a
and
can
do
go
I
like
see
the
to
we
you

DECODING SKILLS TAUGHT TO DATE
Initial and final consonant *m*; short *a*; initial *s*; initial and final consonant *p*; initial and final consonant *t*; initial and medial vowel *i*; initial and final consonant *n*; initial *c*; initial and medial vowel *o*; initial and final *d*

Grade K • Unit 4
www.mheonline.com/readingwonders

978-0-02-131267-2
MHID 0-02-131267-2

EAN

99701

9 780021 312672

**Mc
Graw
Hill**
Education